# Dinosaur Food

Unearth the secrets behind dinosaur fossils

QEB Publishing

Rupert Matthews

# DINOSAUR DIG

Copyright © QEB Publishing 2008

First published in the USA in 2008 by QEB Publishing Inc
3 Wrigley, Suite A
Irvine, CA 92618

www.qeb-publishing.com

Library of Congress Cataloging-in-Publication Data

Matthews, Rupert.
    Dinosaur foods / Rupert Matthews.
       p. cm. -- (Dinosaur dig)
    Includes index.
    ISBN 978-1-59566-551-5
    1. Dinosaurs--Food--Juvenile literature. 2. Paleontology--Triassic--Juvenile literature. 3. Paleontology--Jurassic--Juvenile literature. 4. Paleontology--Cretaceous--Juvenile literature. I. Title.
    QE861.5.M363 2009
    567.9--dc22

2008011534

Printed and bound in the United States of America in North Mankato, Minnesota

092809
QED 10-2009 3

**Author** Rupert Matthews
**Consultant** Neil Clark
**Editor** Amanda Askew
**Designer** Liz Wiffen

**Publisher** Steve Evans
**Creative Director** Zeta Davies

**Picture credits** (t = top, b = bottom, l = left, r = right)
**Alamy** Chris Howes/Wild Places Photography 13
**Corbis** Layne Kennedy 4, Louie Psihoyos 7, Louie Psihoyos 9, Louie Psihoyos 11, Louie Psihoyos 21, Louie Psihoyos 22, Richard Cummins 25, Paul A Souders 27
**Getty Images** Louie Psihoyos 15
**Science Photo Library** Mehau Kulyk 17
**Shutterstock** 2

Words in **bold** can be found in the glossary on page 31.

# CONTENTS

## DINO GUIDE

For every dinosaur in this book and many more, learn how to pronounce their name, find out their length and weight, and discover what they ate.

# DINOSAUR DIG

Dinosaurs **were a group of animals that lived millions of years ago. There were many different types of dinosaur living all over the world.**

Some dinosaurs were enormous, growing to be the largest animals that have ever walked the Earth. Other dinosaurs were much smaller, about the size of a chicken. The last dinosaurs died out around 65 million years ago.

*The strong, sharp teeth of Tyrannosaurus (tie-rann-oh-saw-rus) made this dinosaur a ferocious and successful meat eater.*

1 A dinosaur dies on a lakeshore

2

3 The **skeleton** sinks into the lake

Scientists called **paleontologists** (pay-lee-on-toll-oh-jists) study the remains of dinosaurs, called **fossils**.

By looking at the teeth and jaws of a dinosaur, paleontologists can decide what sort of food it ate. The legs and claws show how it found its food.

⬤ *When a plant or animal dies, it usually rots away completely. However, in special conditions, parts of it can become fossilized.*

## How big were dinosaurs?

Every dinosaur is compared to an average adult, about 5 feet 2 in height, to show just how big they really were.

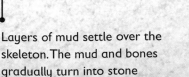

Layers of mud settle over the skeleton. The mud and bones gradually turn into stone

The rock wears away, or **erodes**

As more rock erodes, the skeleton is revealed

# DINOSAUR SNAPPERS

**DIG SITE**

**Some dinosaur hunters were fairly small. They lived by hunting animals that were smaller than themselves.**

They had to be able to move quickly and easily to catch their prey. These hunters could leap and change direction suddenly.

*Staurikosaurus* (store-ick-oh-saw-rus) was a small hunter that ran quickly on its back legs, snapping up food in its mouth. Scientists are not certain to which dinosaur family it belonged.

*Eoraptor* (ee-oh-rap-tor) probably fed on small animals. It would run quickly after its prey and then tear the victim apart with its small, sharp teeth.

*Staurikosaurus*

6.5 feet in length

● *Staurikosaurus would eat anything that it could catch, including large insects.*

● Eoraptor is the earliest known dinosaur. It may have used its sharp claws to dig for food or to grab smaller animals.

Eoraptor

3 feet in length

# WOW!

Eoraptor had small teeth, so it probably only hunted small animals.

◑ A scientist cleans an Eoraptor **skull** to remove the surrounding stone. The process can take weeks and needs great care.

# LIZARD EATERS

Some early dinosaurs, such as *Coelophysis* (see-low-fye-sis), hunted lizards and other small animals, including mammals **and** amphibians.

The skeleton of *Coelophysis* was made up of slender, thin bones that were very light. This enabled *Coelophysis* to move quickly and change direction easily.

The long neck of *Coelophysis* could twist, so that the head could dart forward to snap up prey. The front legs had clawed hands that were used for digging in soil to find food.

## DINOSAUR DIG
### Coelophysis
**WHERE:** New Mexico, North America

**PERIOD:** 225 million years ago in the late Triassic

**DIG SITE**

## WOW!

A *Coelophysis* skull was taken up into space to the *Mir* space station in 1998.

Coelophysis

10 feet in length

⬤ A fossil skeleton of Coelophysis.
It is very rare to find a complete
skeleton with every bone in its place.

⬤ Coelophysis *gulps down a
lizard. Coelophysis would have
eaten small prey whole. Larger prey
would have been torn apart before
being swallowed.*

# PLANT EATERS

Dinosaurs were a very successful group of animals. They soon took over from other types of reptile that had ruled the Earth up until the Triassic Period.

The first dinosaurs were all quite small, but soon larger types began to appear. *Plateosaurus* (plat-ee-oh-saw-rus) was one of the first big plant eaters, growing up to 26 feet in length with a heavy body and thick legs.

◑ Plateosaurus *had jagged, or serrated, teeth that were suited to shredding tough leaves of tree ferns and other large plants of the time.*

## DINOSAUR DIG
### Plateosaurus

**WHERE:** Germany, Europe

**PERIOD:** 215 million years ago in the late Triassic

⚒ **DIG SITE**

*Plateosaurus*

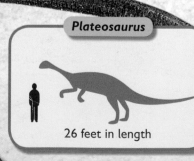

26 feet in length

*Plateosaurus* walked on all four legs most of the time, but could rear up on its back legs to reach leaves at the top of trees.

The front feet had a large claw on the thumb, which may have been used to dig up roots for *Plateosaurus* to eat.

○ *This fossilized skeleton of Plateosaurus has been reconstructed standing upright to show its great size.*

## WOW!

More than 100 fossilized remains of *Plateosaurus* have been found in about 50 different locations.

# DESERT DWELLERS

**The weather during the early Jurassic Period was generally warm and wet.**

There may have also been very dry areas, called **deserts**, or long periods of time without rain, called droughts.

The animals that lived in these areas had to survive in dry conditions as well as in the wet. *Lufengosaurus* (loo-fung-oh-saw-rus) was a plant-eating dinosaur with sharp teeth to shred up tough plant food. The large claws on its front legs helped it to dig for food and water.

**DIG SITE**

◑ Lufengosaurus *could eat tough fernlike plants. Its sharp teeth were ideally suited to this sort of food.*

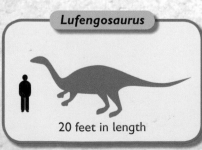

**Lufengosaurus**

20 feet in length

The plants were digested in an enormous stomach, which was positioned in front of the back legs. The weight of its stomach meant that *Lufengosaurus* and similar dinosaurs found it easier to walk on all four legs.

◑ *The fossil skeleton of Lufengosaurus has been reconstructed to rear up. This shows how it used its neck to reach high into a tree to find food.*

## WOW!

Some scientsits believe that the plant eater *Jingshanosaurus* (yin-shahn-oh-saw-rus) may have also eaten shellfish.

**All animals need to drink water in order to survive. Water is used to help chemical processes inside the body.**

Dinosaurs, like all reptiles, had skin that was covered in tough scales. These scales were waterproof and also stopped their body from losing water. Dinosaurs could then store water in their body, so they needed to drink less water than other animals.

## DINOSAUR DIG
### Huayangosaurus
**WHERE:** China, Asia

**PERIOD:** 165 million years ago in the mid Jurassic

**DIG SITE**

*Huayangosaurus*

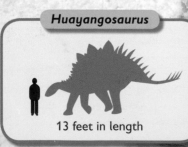

13 feet in length

⬤ Huayangosaurus (hoo-ah-yang-oh-saw-rus) drinks from a stream. This dinosaur lived at a time when the climate was warm and wet, so there was always plenty of water to drink.

# WOW!

The long spines on *Huayangosaurus* are often shown on the shoulder, but it is uncertain where they were positioned.

⬤ A fossil skeleton of Huayangosaurus shows the low position of the head. This allowed the dinosaur to feast on shrubs and other low-growing plants.

# CLEVER FEEDING

Over time, dinosaurs adapted, or changed, so they could find food successfully. Some were quick, some were huge, and others had specialized body parts.

The plant-eating **ornithopod** had a long, muscular tongue to pull leaves into its mouth. The leaves were then bitten off using the sharp beak at the front of its jaws. Finally, the ornithopod chewed the food using strong teeth at the back of its jaws.

**Sauropod** dinosaurs were huge plant eaters with a long neck and tail. They weighed up to 80 tons each and ate a huge amount of plant food every day.

**DINOSAUR DIG**
Camptosaurus
..........................
Haplocanthosaurus
..........................
**WHERE:** Colorado, North America
..........................
**PERIOD:** 150 million years ago in the late Jurassic
..........................

**DIG SITE**

🔵 *Sauropods, such as Haplocanthosaurus (hap-low-kan-thoe-saw-rus) used their weight to push over tall trees, so they could reach the leaves at the top.*

*Haplocanthosaurus*

72 feet in length

◐ A fossil skeleton of Camptosaurus (kamp-toe-saw-rus) shows the dinosaur walking on its back legs, although it could also walk on all four.

◓ *Camptosaurus* had a skull that was long and low compared to that of other similar dinosaurs. This allowed space for hundreds of teeth, which were used to chew up food.

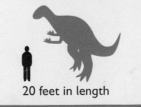

Camptosaurus

20 feet in length

# IN THE UNDERGROWTH

There were small plant eaters as well as giant sauropods. These dinosaurs may have fed in the undergrowth.

Smaller plant eaters had plenty of food because they could feed on shorter plants that larger dinosaurs missed. They could also hide from danger in the undergrowth.

## DINOSAUR DIG
### Micropachy-cephalosaurus

**WHERE:** Shandong, China, Asia

**WHEN:** 77 million years ago in the late Cretaceous

**DIG SITE**

◗ *A pair of Micropachycephalosaurus (my-kro-pak-ee-sef-uh-low-saw-rus) feed while looking out for danger. Micropachycephalosaurus may have had striped skin, so they could blend in, or be camouflaged, with the plants.*

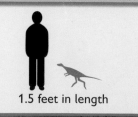

*Micropachycephalosaurus*

1.5 feet in length

*Micropachycephalosaurus* lived among the undergrowth and small plants. They nibbled at leaves and shoots rather than gulping down lots of plant food.

## WOW!

*Micropachycephalosaurus* has the longest name of any dinosaur.

19

# TREE EATERS

Some sauropods had front legs that were much longer than their back legs. They may also have held their neck upright.

The tallest sauropod was *Sauroposeidon* (saw-roh-pos-eye-don). Its body measured 60 feet in height—as tall as two houses! These dinosaurs used their neck to feed on leaves at the top of conifer trees.

*Sauroposeidon* was the last sauropod with long front legs. About 95 million years ago, it became **extinct**.

**DIG SITE**

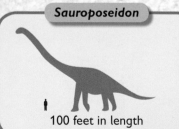

*Sauroposeidon*

100 feet in length

◐ *Sauroposeidon uses its great height to nibble at the top of a conifer tree. Tall trees were out of reach for smaller plant eaters.*

Amargasaurus (ah-mar-gah-saw-rus) was found in Argentina, South America. It may have had flaps of skin connecting the rods of bone that grew up from its neck and back. This was probably used to scare away other dinosaurs.

# WOW!

*Sauroposeidon* was named after the Greek god Poseidon because he was the "Earthshaker," and the Earth probably shook when *Sauroposeidon* moved around.

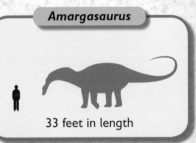

**Amargasaurus**

33 feet in length

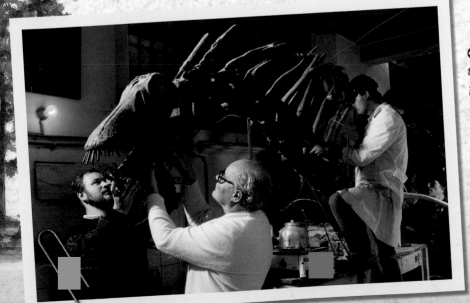

Scientists work to put together a fossilized skeleton of Amargasaurus. Putting the bones into the correct positions is a skilled task.

Some dinosaurs had front legs with special features that were used to help with feeding.

The arms of *Deinocheirus* (day-no-kye-rus) were 8.5 feet in length with hooked claws on the end that were both sharp and strong.

Some paleontologists think that *Deinocheirus* used its claws to hook and pull down tree branches so that it could eat the leaves. Others think that it used them to dig in the ground to find roots or insects.

## DINOSAUR DIG

**Deinocheirus**

**WHERE:** Mongolia, Asia

**WHEN:** 70 million years ago in the late Cretaceous

**DIG SITE**

◗ *Deinocheirus had the largest arms and claws of any dinosaur. The claws would have been even larger than shown here as they were covered in horn.*

# WOW!

Only the arms of *Deinocheirus* have been found. Scientists are not quite certain what the rest of its body looked like.

⬤ Some scientists believe that *Deinocheirus* may have had feathers to keep it warm. Others believe that its skin was actually like that of a reptile.

**Deinocheirus**

36 feet in length

# POWERFUL JAWS

**The very last group of dinosaurs were the** ceratopians. **They had unusual teeth and jaws.**

Very powerful muscles closed the jaws, while the teeth were arranged to slice food up into tiny pieces before it was swallowed. Scientists think that ceratopians, such as *Leptoceratops* (lep-toe-ser-ah-tops), may have feasted on the leaves and twigs of flowering shrubs.

Meat eaters such as *Albertosaurus* (al-bert-oh-saw-rus) had muscles that could clamp the jaws together with great force, but the muscles that opened the jaws were much weaker.

## DINOSAUR DIG

**Albertosaurus**

**Leptoceratops**

**WHERE:** Alberta, North America

**WHEN:** 70 million years ago in the late Cretaceous

**DIG SITE**

⬤ Leptoceratops *fed on small plants. It bit off leaves using its beaklike mouth.*

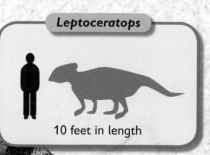

*Leptoceratops*

10 feet in length

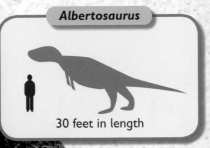

⊖ A fossil skeleton of Albertosaurus is shown with its body bent forward. This gave the dinosaur balance when it walked.

**Albertosaurus**

30 feet in length

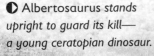

◐ Albertosaurus stands upright to guard its kill— a young ceratopian dinosaur.

# WOW!

In 2000, Philip Currie and his team found 12 Albertosaurus skeletons in Alberta, Canada. This showed that they probably lived and hunted in packs.

# SURVIVAL

**The ceratopian dinosaurs became very successful in North America because the plants on which they fed grew everywhere.**

All ceratopians had beaks that they used to crop plant food and slicing teeth to cut it up before swallowing.

About 65 million years ago, dinosaurs became extinct. It is likely that the plants that plant eaters ate died out, leaving them without any food. Once the plant eaters began to disappear, meat eaters were left with no food either.

## DINOSAUR DIG

Chasmosaurus
..............................
Styracosaurus
..............................
**WHERE:** Alberta, North America
..............................
**WHEN:** 65 million years ago in the late Cretaceous
..............................

**DIG SITE**

◑ *Styracosaurus (sty-rak-oh-saw-rus) feeds on plants on the ground. Scientists have found thousands of Styracosaurus fossils, but only one is of a complete skull.*

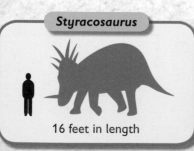

*Styracosaurus*

16 feet in length

## WOW!

Scientists used to think that there had been six species of *Chasmosaurus*, but now they think there were only four.

⬤ The patterned **neck frill** of Chasmosaurus *(kaz-mo-saw-rus) would have been used in threat displays to scare away hunters.*

### Chasmosaurus

20 feet in length

◗ Chasmosaurus *had large holes in its neck frill to lighten the weight on its neck.*

# DINO GUIDE

### Coelophysis (p8)
**PRONUNCIATION**
see-low-fye-sis
**LENGTH** 10 feet
**WEIGHT** 75–80 pounds
**DIET** Small animals

### Mussaurus
**PRONUNCIATION**
muss-saw-rus
**LENGTH** 13 feet (adult)
**WEIGHT** 330 pounds
**DIET** Plants

### Efraasia
**PRONUNCIATION**
ef-rah-see-ah
**LENGTH** 23 feet
**WEIGHT** 1,300 pounds
**DIET** Plants

### Pisanosaurus
**PRONUNCIATION**
peez-an-oh-saw-rus
**LENGTH** 3 feet
**WEIGHT** 6.5 pounds
**DIET** Plants

### Eoraptor (p7)
**PRONUNCIATION**
ee-oh-rap-tor
**LENGTH** 3 feet
**WEIGHT** 7–30 pounds
**DIET** Small animals

### Plateosaurus (p10)
**PRONUNCIATION**
plat-ee-oh-saw-rus
**LENGTH** 26 feet
**WEIGHT** 1 ton
**DIET** Plants

### Herrerasaurus
**PRONUNCIATION**
he-ray-ra-saw-rus
**LENGTH** 10 feet
**WEIGHT** 450 pounds
**DIET** Animals

### Riojasaurus
**PRONUNCIATION**
ree-oh-ha-saw-rus
**LENGTH** 33 feet
**WEIGHT** 1 ton
**DIET** Plants

### Melanorosaurus
**PRONUNCIATION**
mel-an-or-oh-saw-rus
**LENGTH** 33 feet
**WEIGHT** 1 ton
**DIET** Plants

### Staurikosaurus (p6)
**PRONUNCIATION**
store-ick-oh-saw-rus
**LENGTH** 6.5 feet
**WEIGHT** 65 pounds
**DIET** Small animals

# JURASSIC PERIOD
## 206 TO 145 MILLION YEARS AGO

## Allosaurus
**PRONUNCIATION**
al-oh-saw-rus
**LENGTH** 40 feet
**WEIGHT** 1.5 - 2 tons
**DIET** Animals

## Anchisaurus
**PRONUNCIATION**
an-kee-saw-rus
**LENGTH** 8 feet
**WEIGHT** 75 pounds
**DIET** Plants

## Apatosaurus
**PRONUNCIATION**
ap-at-oh-saw-rus
**LENGTH** 82 feet
**WEIGHT** 25–35 tons
**DIET** Plants

## Camptosaurus (p16)
**PRONUNCIATION**
kamp-toe-saw-rus
**LENGTH** 20 feet
**WEIGHT** 1–2 tons
**DIET** Plants

## Coelurus
**PRONUNCIATION**
seel-yur-rus
**LENGTH** 6.5 feet
**WEIGHT** 35 pounds
**DIET** Animals

## Haplocanthosaurus (p16)
**PRONUNCIATION**
hap-low-kan-thoe-saw-rus
**LENGTH** 72 feet
**WEIGHT** 20 tons
**DIET** Plants

## Huayangosaurus (p14)
**PRONUNCIATION**
hoo-ah-yang-oh-saw-rus
**LENGTH** 13 feet
**WEIGHT** 880–1,300 pounds
**DIET** Plants

## Jingshanosaurus (p13)
**PRONUNCIATION**
yin-shahn-oh-saw-rus
**LENGTH** 25 feet
**WEIGHT** 1 ton
**DIET** Plants

## Lufengosaurus (p12)
**PRONUNCIATION**
loo-fung-oh-saw-rus
**LENGTH** 20 feet
**WEIGHT** 500 pounds
**DIET** Plants

## Ornitholestes
**PRONUNCIATION**
or-nith-oh-less-teez
**LENGTH** 6.5 feet
**WEIGHT** 65 pounds
**DIET** Animals

# CRETACEOUS PERIOD
## 145 TO 65 MILLION YEARS AGO

### Albertosaurus (p25)

**PRONUNCIATION** al-bert-oh-saw-rus
**LENGTH** 30 feet
**WEIGHT** 2.5 tons
**DIET** Animals

### Amargasaurus (p21)

**PRONUNCIATION** ah-mar-gah-saw-rus
**LENGTH** 33 feet
**WEIGHT** 5–7 tons
**DIET** Plants

### Chasmosaurus (p26)

**PRONUNCIATION** kaz-mo-saw-rus
**LENGTH** 20 feet
**WEIGHT** 2–3 tons
**DIET** Plants

### Deinocheirus (p22)

**PRONUNCIATION** day-no-kye-rus
**LENGTH** 36 feet
**WEIGHT** 4–7 tons
**DIET** Animals and plants

### Leptoceratops (p24)

**PRONUNCIATION** lep-toe-ser-ah-tops
**LENGTH** 10 feet
**WEIGHT** 100–450 pounds
**DIET** Plants

### Micropachycephalosaurus (p18)
**PRONUNCIATION** my-kro-pak-ee-sef-uh-low-saw-rus
**LENGTH** 1.5 feet
**WEIGHT** 45 pounds
**DIET** Plants

### Sauroposeidon (p20)
**PRONUNCIATION** saw-roh-pos-eye-don
**LENGTH** 100 feet
**WEIGHT** 50–80 tons
**DIET** Plants

### Stygimoloch

**PRONUNCIATION** stij-ee-mol-ock
**LENGTH** 6.5–10 feet
**WEIGHT** 150–450 pounds
**DIET** Plants

### Styracosaurus (p26)

**PRONUNCIATION** sty-rak-oh-saw-rus
**LENGTH** 16 feet
**WEIGHT** 3 tons
**DIET** Plants

### Tyrannosaurus (p4)

**PRONUNCIATION** tie-rann-oh-saw-rus
**LENGTH** 40 feet
**WEIGHT** 6 tons
**DIET** Large animals

# GLOSSARY

**Amphibian** An animal that lays its eggs in water, but lives most of its life on land.

**Ceratopian** A group of dinosaurs that had a neck frill and teeth designed for slicing. Most ceratopians also had horns on their head.

**Cretaceous** The third period of time in the age of the dinosaurs. The Cretaceous began about 145 million years ago and ended about 65 million years ago.

**Desert** A very dry area of land where few, if any, plants or animals live.

**Dinosaur** A type of reptile that lived millions of years ago. All dinosaurs are now extinct.

**Erode** To wear away.

**Extinct** Not existing any more. An animal is extinct when they have all died out.

**Fossil** Any part of a plant or animal that has been preserved in rock. Also traces of plants or animals, such as footprints.

**Jurassic** The second period of time in the age of the dinosarus. The Jurassic began about 206 million years ago and ended about 145 million years ago.

**Mammal** An animal that has hair or fur and produces milk for its babies.

**Neck frill** A thin plate of bone and skin growing from the back of an animal's skull.

**Ornithopod** A group of plant-eating dinosaurs that had a beak and strong chewing teeth.

**Paleontologist** A scientist who studies ancient forms of life, including dinosaurs.

**Reptile** A cold-blooded animal, such as a lizard. Dinosaurs were reptiles, too.

**Sauropod** A type of dinosaur that had a long neck and tail. Sauropods included the largest of all dinosaurs.

**Skeleton** The bones in an animal's body.

**Skull** The bones of the head of an animal. The skull does not include the jaw, but many skulls have jaws attached.

**Triassic** The first period of time in the age of the dinosaurs. The Triassic began about 248 million years ago and ended about 208 million years ago.

# INDEX